PROJECT MANAGEMENT

Forms and Checklists for Project Managers

Andreas Ketter

Content

Preface

Checklists and forms support a structured approach to analysis, evaluation, action plans, controls and decision-making. They are also helpful when preparing negotiations, presentations, reports and meetings. Tasks can be defined, standardized and simplified with the help of forms and checklists, leading to improved quality management.

Thorough preparation and planning are the best prerequisites for the successful realization of projects.

The forms and checklists listed below can and should be adjusted to fit the actual project situation and content to ensure the greatest success.

Many basic questions and checks are already in place. It is up to you as a user to decide what to change, supplement or omit.

Depending on the project category (complexity, size, cross-border activities, etc.), more or less checks may be required to achieve the desired result.

Basic questions such as the availability of a written order should always be clarified in advance. Other questions such as licensing rights and security issues may not be relevant for many projects. The project manager must decide on a case-by-case basis. It is helpful to prepare different versions in advance (e.g., simple, normal, complex) for certain checklists and forms that will be used repeatedly and improved upon or updated. Having such templates in place will be a great timesaving measure.

Order Checklist

The following checklist assumes that a written order exists. It aims to analyze this order and the related documents. Based on this analysis you can determine the basic plan and actions needed to define it more clearly. Furthermore, insights may be gained by analyzing risk and opportunity management.

Description	Status
Project plan available?	
Delivery and scope of service completely described?	
All interfaces defined and unambiguously described?	
Scope and content for support and training described?	
Requirements for documentation defined?	
Open points to be clarified?	
Involvement of the customer defined?	
Change request management process defined?	
Risk and opportunity management plan available?	
Escalation management defined?	
(Partial) Acceptance process agreed?	
Problem reporting procedure defined?	
Payment plan, billing process and indexation defined?	
Agreement in case of delay defined?	
Warranty periods and process defined?	
Limitation of liability agreed?	
Collateral, guarantees and solvency test available?	
Licensing rights regulated?	
Disclosure clause existing?	
Contract term fixed?	

Description	Status
Regulations and definition for force majeure clause in place?	
Transfer and transfer of rights and obligations defined?	
Arrangement for possible subsidiary agreements in place?	
Jurisdiction/Applicable law established?	
Severance clause included?	
Sequence/priority of documents and annexes defined?	

Document Checklist

To guarantee good planning and project execution, it is necessary to have a complete overview on the related documents and their status. The project manager must know whether and which documents are missing and if the existing documents are up to date and complete. Only then can he or she create an action plan in which it is established who carries out various actions related to the document status. This makes a detailed project status easily available to all project participants and the checklist documents the next steps to be taken in the project. (Not all documents mentioned in such a checklist are always required. This is explained in the document overview.)

For documents that are regularly updated, e.g., the opportunity and risk overview, someone should be appointed to be responsible for seeing that all actions are initiated, monitored and reported. This can be done in the document overview sheet in the field "comments." Then it is clear to all who is responsible for this document and with what frequency the updating of the document takes place. Only the status summary is entered into the document overview. Individual actions and detail status are recorded, monitored and controlled by additional action plans.

Color-coding status details (available, up to date, complete) can help in capturing overall status at a glance. With the next update of this checklist, it becomes immediately apparent if changes have occurred and, if so, what those changes are.

Since the number of documents is frequently extensive, this checklist can best be recorded and evaluated in a database such as Excel.

Document Checklist

Project Name	YYYYYYYYYYYYYY			a)	35%	7 out of 20 documents are not available	Project Manager **John Doe**
Project Number	**XXXXXXXXXXXXXXX**	**P** **M**		b)	46%	6 out of 13 documents are not up-to-date	Phone +xx xxxxxx xxxxxxxx
		PROFI		c)	69%	9 out of 13 documents are not complete	E-Mail j.doe@muster.com

	Documents	a)	b)	c)	**Notes**
1.0	**Project Contract / Order**				
1.1	**Milestones**				
1.2	**Project Deadline**				
1.3	**Project Schedule**				
1.4	**Interface Definition / Demarcation**				
1.5	**Payment Plan**				
1.6	**Opportunities & Risics Analysis**				
1.7	**Stakeholder Analysis**				
1.8	**SWOT Analysis**				
1.9	**Organisation Plan (internally)**				
1.10	**Organisation Plan (extenally)**				
1.11	**Communication Plan**				
1.12	**Reporting Structur**				
1.13	**Status Reporting**				
1.14	**Drawings**				
1.15	**List of Deliverables & Requirements**				
1.16	**Guidelines & Regulations**				
1.17	**Project Description / Profile (short)**				
1.18	**Project Manager Target Agreement**				
1.19	**Project Team Member Target**				
1.20	**...**				

Color green: available, up-to-date, complete
Colorred: not available, not up-to-date, not complete

Project Start-Up Checklist

During the project start-up workshop, the participants should be able to get a clear picture of the project objectives, timeline, organization and roles, communication and information, rules and processes. At the end of this workshop, the participants should make a commitment about the agreed topics and the best way to run the project.

A number of items should be prepared in advance, to ensure an effective meeting and efficient workshop. These topics are included in the following checklist:

1. Project description, objectives and benefits
2. Project contents, structure and interfaces
3. Dates and milestones
4. Project budget and order calculation and project controls
5. Opportunities and risks
6. SWOT analysis
7. Organization and team
8. Project environment and stakeholders
9. Project reviews
10. Project status reports
11. Communication and escalation
12. Specific requirements and rules
13. Other remarks

Open points: to be clarified/open action items	Responsible	until when

The General Project Plan

During the project kick-off the main elements of the project were identified and various points were worked out together. Team members were asked to do further detailed work.

The target is to incorporate all those results into the project plan, so that all parties have the same up-to-date information about the project.

The project plan is not a static document; it must be updated and completed regularly.

The project plan has to be approved and released by the internal customer. This marks the official start of the project.

Therefor the cover sheet should be signed and contain the minimum information stated below.

As the project plan is continually updated, the actually valid version of the project plan should be available as an online document. Thus everyone involved can use the current version and misunderstandings of obsolete documents can be avoided.

Cover sheet for the project plan

Project name:				
Order number:				
Distribution list:	Name	Function	E-Mail	Phone
Created by:	John Doe, Project Manager			
Date:		Signature:		
Released by:	Frank Boss, Head of Division			
Date:		Signature:		

Project plan content

Project description	**Dates and Milestones**
Client/Contact persons	Project start/Project end
Project Scope (in/out of scope)	Project phases (start/end)
Project objectives/benefits	Milestones/acceptance and approval

Costs

Quality, Environment Health Safety (EHS)

Total value	Quality Requirements
Material/Labor costs	Quality Management
Internal/External costs	EHS Requirements
Payment plan/billing process	EHS Management

Information/Communication	**Project Organization**
Meetings internal/external	Project team internal/external
Status reports	Responsibilities/authorizations
Controlling/monitoring	Roles/target agreements

Environment/Stakeholder/SWOT Analysis

Direct project environment: Interests, possible support and resistances, strengths and weaknesses (internal/external)
Indirect project environment: Interests, possible support and resistances, strengths and weaknesses (internal/external)

Opportunities and Risks

Opportunities: likelihood of occurrence, impact, measure
Risks: likelihood of occurrence, impact, measure

Experiences and insights from other projects (lessons learned) should always be included in the project plan.

Example of a Detailed Project Plan

Client	International Test Inc.
Contact person Client	John Denver +1 xxx john.denver@intertest.com
Project Manager	PM PROFI +1 xxx pm.profi@me.com
Commercial Project Manager	PM PROFI +1 xxx pm.profi@me.com
Project name Project number	PMP International Test Project 2017-99-7834
Project start Project end	October 1, 2017 March 31, 2018
Project value Project category	$65M USD Complex

Project Description (short)

Turnkey Order
- New office building with 45 floors and underground parking area
- Connection to the public utilities network, energy supply and distribution in and to the building, emergency power supply
- Indoor and outdoor lighting, security technology, building automation, fire protection technology, access control, IT network

Option
- Data center and IT hardware, decision to be taken within the next 2-3 months

Revision Log

Changes to the document "Project plan"

Revision Log				
Rev	**Author**	**Date**	**Chapter**	**Changes**
1				
2				
3				

1 Project History

All relevant events and results since initial project quote, specifically, documentation of the sales phase and contract negotiations are recorded here. Use lessons learned from completed projects and consider the entries in your Customer Relation Management (CRM) System.

2 Project Overview

2.1 Project scope		Link
Project Name	PMP International Test Project	>>Link <<
Energy	Complete energy supply and distribution	>>Link <<
Emergency Power Supply	Diesel, transformer, main power distribution cabinet	>>Link <<
Interior Lighting	Offices, corridors, emergency lighting, etc.	>>Link <<
Outdoor Lighting	Functional and decorative	>>Link <<
Security Technology and Access Control	Camera surveillance	>>Link <<
Fire Fighting Equipment	>>Description<<	>>Link <<
Building Automation	>>Description<<	>>Link <<
Others	>>Description<<	>>Link <<

2.2 Site information		Link
Location	>>Enter Location<<	>>Link <<
Address	>>Enter Address<<	>>Link <<
Location (Map): >>Insert photo or drawing or a map<<		>>Link <<
Layout: >>Insert detail photos or detail drawing of the construction site<<		>>Link <<

2.3 Customer information		Link
Contracting party	>> Enter Name<<	>>Link <<
Organizational plan, customer		>>Link <<
List of customer contacts		>>Link <<

2.4 Internal project organization	Link
Organizational plan	>>Link <<
List of internal contacts	>>Link <<

2.5 Main supplier		Link
Transformers	>>Supplier Name<<	>>Link <<
Emergency power generator	>>Supplier Name<<	>>Link <<
Foundation and building	>>Supplier Name<<	>>Link <<
Streets and access paths	>>Supplier Name<<	>>Link <<
Office lighting	>>Supplier Name<<	>>Link <<
Security systems	>>Supplier Name<<	>>Link <<
Fire protection systems	>>Supplier Name<<	>>Link <<
Power cable	>>Supplier Name<<	>>Link <<
Others	>>Supplier Name<<	>>Link <<

2.6 Sub supplier (from customer and suppliers)		Link
>>Description<<	>>Name of Sub Supplier<<	>>Link <<

2.7 Production of components			Link
Component	Production Site	Shipping Route	
>>Description<<	>>Description<<	>>Description<<	>>Link <<

3 Important Agreements

3.1 Contract and important details		Link
Main contract	Signed by >>Insert Name or Organization<<	>>Link <<
Service and maintenance contract	Signed by >>Insert Name or Organization<<	>>Link <<
Other contracts	Signed by >>Insert Name or Organization<<	>>Link <<
Contractual obligations	List of obligations (from the sales phase) updated by project manager	>>Link <<
Date of contract signature	>>Insert Date<<	

Project start date	>>Insert Date<<	
Start production and assembly	>>Insert Date<<	
Construction phase	>>Insert Date<<	
Commissioning phase	>>Insert Date<<	
Handover phase	>>Insert Date<<	

3.2 Contract modifications/additions	Link
>>Insert all agreed adjustments<<	>>Link <<

3.3 Changing orders from the original contract	Link
Changes in orders must be discussed during the project status meetings.	>>Link <<

3.4 Technology	Link
>>List all essential technical features<<	>>Link <<

3.5 Project checklist	Link
The project checklist contains the technical details of all components and parts to be supplied and serves as base for the spare parts list.	>>Link <<

3.6 Guarantee and warranty		Link
Products, components, systems	>>Description<<	>>Link <<
Others	>>Description<<	>>Link <<

3.7 Construction schedule	Link
>>Insert Link or Picture<<	>>Link <<

3.8 Payment plan	Link
>>Description of the contractually agreed payment terms and conditions<<	>>Link <<

3.9 Penalties and bonus/malus agreements	Link
>>Description<<	>>Link <<

3.10 Documentation	Link
>>Description of contractual agreements<<	>>Link <<

4   Project Plans

4.1 EHS	Link
EHS plan of the customer	>>Link <<
EHS plan internal	>>Link <<
EHS targets for the project	>>Link <<

4.2 Quality	Link
Quality plan of the customer	>>Link <<
Quality plan internal	>>Link <<
Quality targets for the project	>>Link <<

4.3 Communication	Link
Communication plan external	>>Link <<
Communication plan internal	>>Link <<

4.4 Claim strategy	Link
>>Description of the claim strategy<<	>>Link <<

4.5 Escalation plan	Link
>>Insert names of the steering committee members and description of the escalation plan<<	>>Link <<

4.6 Reporting		Link
Internal	Monthly/weekly project status meeting including budget review and cost controlling	>>Link <<
External	Project progress report according to contract (usually monthly); other reports, if additionally agreed on with the customer	>>Link <<

4.7 Insurance plan	Link
>>Description<<	>>Link <<

4.8 Production	Link
Production schedule	>>Link <<
Factory acceptance	>>Link <<

4.9 Transportation		Link
Transportation plan	>>Description<<	>>Link <<
Mode of transport	>>Description<<	>>Link <<

4.10 Opportunities and risks		Link
Opportunities and risks overview	The project team identifies and assesses opportunities and risks; defines measures and monitors them. Opportunities and risks are additionally updated in regular separate meetings.	>>Link <<

4.11 Stakeholder management		Link
Stakeholder analysis	The project team identifies and assesses the key stakeholders; defines measures and monitors them. The stakeholder analysis is additionally updated in regular separate meetings.	>>Link <<

5 List of Planning Documents

To ensure version control, the project documentation should be stored electronically.

Type	Detail	Link
Site description		>> Link<<
Production plan		>> Link<<
Transportation plan		>> Link<<
Construction and installation plan		>> Link<<
Work instructions		>> Link<<
Installation schedule		>> Link<<
Contract parties/ contractual relations		>> Link<<
Internal organization plan		>> Link<<
Site organization plan, attendance list		>> Link<<

Type	Detail	Link
Phone list		>> Link<<
Project schedule		>> Link<<
Shipping plan		>> Link<<
Commissioning plan		>> Link<<
Commissioning schedule		>> Link<<
EHS plan	Health Safety Environment	>> Link<<
Quality plan		>> Link<<
Commercial documents	• Payment Plan • Budget • Opportunities and risk overview • Claim management and contractual changes • Order intake calculation	>> Link<<
Site reports		>> Link<<
Overview of all scheduled meetings		>> Link<<
Acceptance and handover documents		>> Link<<
Key documents	• Project reporting and controlling • WBS elements, project schedule • Quality management plan	>> Link<<
Type	**Detail**	**Link**
Service and maintenance plan	• Standards, guidelines, process descriptions • Personnel and material planning • Essential components and critical parts • Equipment • Project-specific templates • FAQs and rules for handling special situations	>> Link<<

6   Work Breakdown Structure (WBS) and Organization

In the example below, the project is broken down into four work streams (i.e., sub projects) with four nominated responsible persons. Each of them is responsible for the work package deliverables therein (with respect to deadlines, cost and quality).

All necessary steps/activities/output must be defined within these work packages.

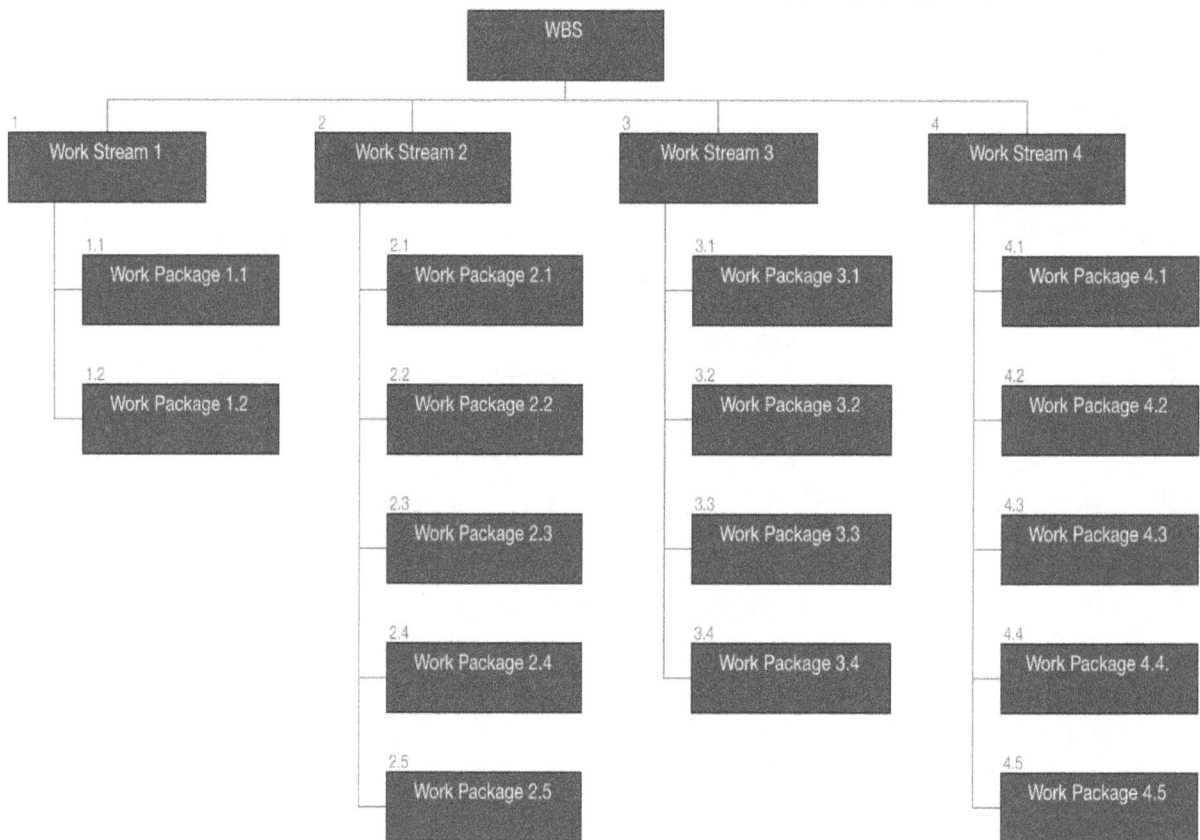

WBS			
1 Work Stream 1	**2** Work Stream 2	**3** Work Stream 3	**4** Work Stream 4
1.1 Work Package 1.1	2.1 Work Package 2.1	3.1 Work Package 3.1	4.1 Work Package 4.1
1.2 Work Package 1.2	2.2 Work Package 2.2	3.2 Work Package 3.2	4.2 Work Package 4.2
	2.3 Work Package 2.3	3.3 Work Package 3.3	4.3 Work Package 4.3
	2.4 Work Package 2.4	3.4 Work Package 3.4	4.4 Work Package 4.4.
	2.5 Work Package 2.5		4.5 Work Package 4.5

7 Attachments

7.1 Performance description/demarcation

This is a detailed description including drawings, photos, etc. It must be clear what the customer provides and what you, as the contractor, have to provide.

7.2 Interfaces description/demarcation

A detailed description of all interfaces must be created to avoid misunderstandings and delays in execution.

Project Manager Target Agreement

To ensure clarity and understanding between the internal contractor (this could, for example, be the head of project management or the head of sales) and the project manager, a written project manager target agreement is recommended. Here the mutual expectations, duties and authorities as well as assessment criteria for the results to be delivered are agreed upon. (See example below.)

Runtime and category of the project			
Project start		**Project end (planned)**	
Project category	**Small, medium, high/complex**		

Responsibilities and authorities			
Start of the agreement		**End of the agreement (planned)**	
Project manager responsibilities	• Support during offer and negotiation period • Total responsibility for the execution, commissioning, handover and acceptance of all deliverables and services • Ensure technical and commercial success of the project, including cost management and profit optimization • Planning and execution, onsite review, onsite inspections • Managing and coaching of team members • Perform regular project reviews, including documentation and forwarding of the "lessons learned" • Ensure target-oriented communication within the team and with all relevant stakeholders • Continuous project controlling and regular reporting **(to be defined in detail: frequency and form to be used)** • Perform regular Project Status Review Meetings with the head of project management (or head of sales) and separate Lessons Learned Workshops **(to be defined in detail: frequency and minimum agenda and process and form to be used)** • Opportunity and risk management (identify, assess, initiate and monitor actions) including regular updates **(to be defined in detail: frequency and form to be used)** • Escalation management notification of the project manager if any agreed objective of the project is jeopardized. (For example, possible negative impact on the project's profit, contract schedule or desired project quality) • Project administration, per the existing rules • Commissioning, coordination and monitoring/controlling of all project-related internal organizational units and subcontractors • Subcontractor management: tendering and contracting, coordination and monitoring		

Responsibilities and authorities	
Project manager authority	• Makes the necessary decisions (according to internal rules and guidelines), to prevent/mitigate project and/or department losses and damages (within the scope of thresholds defined in this agreement) • Delegates tasks according to existing rules and regulations • Acts, escalates and signs according to the project-specific signature scheme • Gives functional instructions to assigned project team members • Must be consulted before vacations of assigned employees with approval by respective line manager • Maintains right to escalate to next level, if neither the head of project management nor the head of sales respond to escalations within the agreed period of time • Assesses results, skills and potential of the assigned project staff; communication of same to the respective superior • Defines and organizes training for employees within the project framework • Must be consulted and participates in the decision-making process if employees are to be assigned to tasks outside the project • Defines competencies needed within the project team • Participates in selection process for project team members • Has right to independent decision about change requests up to an amount of: *"to be defined"* • Has right to independent decision regarding project costs up to: **"to be defined"**
Head of project management/sales responsibilities	• Authorizes and empowers project managers for project execution • Assigns partial responsibility (e.g., responsibility for project result, transfer of technical authority to act as supervisor for assigned project staff) for duration of the project • Participates in internal and external steering committees • Makes quick decisions in case of problems, escalations and crises • Reacts within the agreed timeframe for escalations • Controls/monitors overall corporate responsibility • Defines strategies and timely communication • Supports the project manager with all resources, specifically with regard to timely decision-making and authorizations • Establishes and approves the claim strategy and enforcement claims against the customers and/or subcontractors • Ensures the qualifications of assigned project staff members according to project requirements • Provides necessary equipment and premises for the project • Conducts project status meetings • Monitors compliance with all internal guidelines • Communicates all project-related information with the project manager • Analyses and communicates of "lessons learned" • Ensures that required resources are available to the project manager • End of the project: the heads of project management/sales relieve the project manager at the final project meeting

Responsibilities and authorities	
Head of project management/sales authorities	• Point of escalation in case of exceeding budget thresholds or if schedule and quality are threatened • Defines internal strategy and priorities within the existing project portfolio • Entitled to up-to-date information about project status at any time • Entitled to make significant changes relating to project objectives • Maintains authority to approve project plans • Entitled to convene internal or external steering committee meetings

Enclosures	Available	Not available	Document name/content/storage location
Documentation			
Offer and contract documents			
Calculations and financial documents			
Project plan			
Organization scheme			
Opportunities and risk analysis			
Claim strategy			
Further documents			

The signatory parties hereby agree to the appointment of the project manager and confirm the functional competencies and responsibilities of this position as described below:

Appointment of the project manager			
Parties	Name	Date	Signature
Head of project management/sales			
Project manager			

The signatory parties hereby agree to dismissal of the project manager as well as the termination of their described functional competencies and responsibilities:

Dismissal of the project manager			
Parties	**Name**	**Date**	**Signature**
Head of project management/sales			
Project manager			

Individual Target Agreement

Using personal project-specific goals provides individual objective criteria for assessing the results achieved by the project manager. These goals can then, for example, be used to determine a possible financial reward to the project manager and/or for the planning of the next steps in his or her professional career.

Project-specific targets for the project manager			
Field	**Weight**	**Score**	**Target definition and description**
Financial	25%	50%	Target project profit in X% or improvement compared to order entry calculation in y%
		25%	Keeping cost for engineering, installation and commissioning within calculated budget
		25%	Target profit in Z% for claims and additional orders
Time	15%	33%	Get commitment to deadlines with stakeholders
		33%	Get commitment to changes in deadlines with stakeholders
		33%	Keeping project progress within planning
Quality	15%	33%	Maximum number of changes due to circumstances for which the company of the PM is responsible
		33%	Coordinate and agree on the planning of all actions to guarantee handover without problems and commitment to the list of open points with all stakeholders
		33%	Max X% deviation from basic project plan
Team	10%	50%	Coaching of team members
		15%	Kick-off meeting with the project team
		35%	Executing reviews and lessons learned workshops on a regular basis and sharing results with all team members
Customer	25%	50%	X% customer satisfaction with regard to the project manager's performance and collaboration
		25%	X% customer satisfaction with regard to project deliveries and services
		25%	X% customer satisfaction with regard to the realized dates
Processes	10%	50%	Accuracy of forecasting total costs and deadlines in progress reports
		50%	Results of action concerning stakeholder management

Preparing Negotiations

Many negotiations (internal and external) are required to guarantee the successful completion of all project tasks. Investing time in a thorough preparation prior to such negotiations is a crucial factor for success.

In order to be fully informed about a given project, it often suffices to read all contract-related documents along with conducting some additional research on the Internet. Sometimes it becomes necessary to have additional personal communication with stakeholders and others outside the project.

It is wise to begin preparation at an early stage and to document all information gained for further use during the course of the project and also to make your information, experience and conclusions available to others involved.

If you already have a long-term relationship with clients and sub suppliers or your company strives for such a relationship, a structured database is a good tool for this purpose.

Finding competencies

Get an accurate picture of the competencies of your negotiation partners.
Learn as much as possible about the people involved in the negotiation.

1. Who will sit at the negotiation table?

2. What are the formal titles and areas of responsibility of the participants?

3. Age and period of company affiliation, relevant experience?

4. What is the corporate structure (hierarchical with strong decision-makers on the top or decentralized)?

5. What is the position and reputation of your negotiating partners in their company? Will they be heard and respected? Try to get information from contacts outside the company.

Your own competencies: What power do you have for negotiation and agreements?

Only by your superior's pre-approved conditions?
If yes, please describe. If you have the power to agree to better conditions, what conditions would be seen as "better" by your superiors?

Only agreements that achieve certain objectives? Describe the goals.
Are you allowed to freely negotiate the details?

Do your superiors want to check and release your negotiation results?

Are your powers limited in USD values, but not with respect to other creative options with no significant financial impact?

Are you authorized to provide information about the needs, interests and preferences of your company if the negotiating partner is interested in a counter-transaction based on the principle of utmost good faith?

Identifying positions and interests

What do you know about your negotiating partners? What is their best alternative to a negotiated agreement? What are your negotiating partners' basic interests and what are their absolute limits at which they would accept an agreement?

To learn as much as possible about the interests and concerns of your negotiating partners have you ...

1. Contacted sources within the business branches?

2. Checked potentially relevant annual reports?

3. Reviewed their balance sheets?

4. Had informal meetings with your negotiating partners and other related persons?

5. Put yourself in the role of your negotiation partners and then considered what their interests, needs and preferences would be?

What do you know ...

about the actual business situation of your negotiation partners?

How good is their financial performance?

What is their strategy?

Which key initiatives does their company follow?

How big is their competitive pressure?

about the value this deal has for your business partner?

How important is this business for your negotiating partners?
Do they need the business with you to achieve a bigger goal and what is this?

about the existence of an alternative business/agreement?

Are there others who can make a comparable offer to your negotiation partners?

Are your negotiation partners able to make an agreement with another business partner and still keep their own deadlines?

Do your negotiation partners already have offers from others or do they already have informal meetings with other parties?

about the conditions your negotiating partners would like to agree on regarding the business you want to close?

What business objectives would be supported by an agreement with you?
Which parts of the agreement could be complicated for the business growth of your partner?
What conditions can you offer that will provide a benefit to your negotiating partner while requiring no major concessions for you?

Project Status Report

For controls and for internal and external reporting it is necessary to determine the status and progress of the project on a regularly basis.

Status reports also serve as a basis for the intervention of the project leader, the establishment of measures and for decision-making.

The better the reports or the listed key performance indicators match the current project, the faster deviations can be detected. Better decisions can be determined and the right measures can be taken.

Therefore, it is useful to prepare the project status report with the stakeholders in advance and to determine how the measured values contained therein will be defined objectively and verifiably.

The following example contains important elements for the above mentioned use in project management. It covers a wide variety.

In a specific case these elements can be modified correspondingly and/or additional elements can be inserted.

Based on this report the project manager will be able to decide which elements might require a more detailed inquiry.

He/she can for example:
- ask for further detailed information
- can plan meetings with experts and people involved
- initiate problem solutions
- initiate an escalation

Essential to this kind of reporting is that it focuses on capturing, evaluating and controlling deviations from the planning.

Project Status Report

Report Period: Year-Month-Date - Year-Month-Date

Project: Test Project	Project Manager: John Doe	E-mail: j.doe@doe.com

Results

Situation: set point/actual value	Deviations: absolute/relative and cumulative	Causes for deviations	Consequences/ measures/impact of measures	Trend/Forecast
1. Dates				
2. Costs				
3. Risks				
4. Customer satisfaction				

Specific problems/situations, consequences/effects, measures and impact of measures

	Problem	Effect	Measures	Impact of measures
1				
2				
3				
4				

Important decisions

Already taken	To be taken	By whom	Until

Changes to order, planning, etc.

Next steps

	Actions for improvements to be taken	By whom	Until
1			
2			

Notes

Opportunities and Risks

Each project carries opportunities and risks. Failures of employees, inadequate competencies, misunderstandings regarding the requirements, calculation errors, etc., are examples of internal risks. Additional project requirements by the client create external opportunities and risks.

Also, outside the direct project environment, e.g., through changes in laws and regulations, currency exchange rate changes, changes in the behavior of the users or by demands of initiatives and associations, situations can arise which can have a significant influence on the project progress and result.

For these reasons, it is advisable to identify the opportunities and risks with the whole project team, to assess them and to decide whether and which measures are necessary to reduce/avoid risks and to increase/secure opportunities.

During the course of a project, new opportunities and risks may arise, requiring reassessment of the previously identified opportunities and risks.

Therefore, active opportunities and risk management requires updating on a regular basis, monitoring of the corresponding measures and, if necessary, adjustment of such measures.

For this purpose, incorporating the use of an Excel file or another database file can be an immense organizational help.

In order to make a realistic forecast of the financial project results, all opportunities and risks need to be integrated into the project calculation and controls.

Opportunities and Risks

Project Name	Test Project		Project Manager	John Doe		
Project Number	xxxxxxxx		Phone	+yyxxxxxx xxxxxx		
Date	xx.xx.xxxx		E-mail	john.doe@doe.com		
Risks	Risk description	Probability %	Impact in $	Measures	Costs of measures	Risk after measures
1. Categorie						
Risk 1						
Risk 2						
Risk 3						
2. Categorie						
Risk 1						
Risk 2						
3. Categorie						
Risk 1						
Risk 2						
.....						
Opportunities	Opportunity description	Probability %	Impact in $	Measures	Costs of measures	Opportunity after measures
1. Categorie						
Opportunity 1						
Opportunity 2						
2. Categorie						
Opportunity 1						
Opportunity 2						
Opportunity 3						
3. Categorie						
Opportunity 1						
Opportunity 2						
Opportunity 3						
.....						

The checklist can be easily added to determine the total risk/opportunities. The probabilities are multiplied by effects and the resulting "relative effects" are added up.

For this purpose, it also makes sense to determine the new probabilities "after taking measures," since the probability of such occurrences arises as a result of taking measures.

Stakeholder Analysis

The progress of the project and the final achievable project result are significantly influenced by various stakeholders. Here it is necessary to identify individual interests, whether these are conducive to or detrimental to the project's objectives, and how influential individual stakeholders may be.

Afterward, it can be decided if and which measures are necessary and meaningful, in order to increase positive influences and reduce negative ones. This analysis should also be updated on a regular basis and the results included in the overview of opportunities and risks.

The following Excel form explains how the evaluation is done. By multiplying the importance of a stakeholder with his/her personal influence, the individual weighing factor is determined.

Based on this, decisions on the need for action are made and the appropriate actions can be defined.

Stakeholder Analysis

Project Manager	John Doe						November 10, 2018		P PROFI
Phone	+yy xxxxxx xxxxxx					E-Mail	john.doe@doe.com		
Project	Test Project					Project Number		xxxxxxxxxxx	

	high								
	medium								
	low								

Stakeholder's Name	Ranking	Stakeholder's Function	Stakeholder's Main Interest	Stakeholder's Importance	Impact Description	Impact Severity	Action	Responsible	Deadline YYYY-MM-DD
	48			8		6			
	54			9		6			
	70			10		7			
	20			5		4			

Problem Solving

If everything goes according to plan, the project manager does not have much to do after creating the project plan.

But as a project grows in complexity and running time, the project leader is confronted with a significant number of challenges. Small and large, expected and unexpected.

Therefore, the topic of problem solving will be discussed here.

Problem solving

In order to solve a problem, it is necessary to first obtain a description of what is considered a problem and to do this as accurately as possible.

Description: What does not work, what is the undesirable result, etc.

Location: Where did the problem occur, in which process: process step, system, unit, part, etc.

Time: When did the problem first occur, when in the process, when does it recur, etc.

Scope: What are the effects of the problem, what is the extent of the problem

Demarcation of the problem

Here it is helpful to ask, "what is" and "what is not"

That is, what is affected and what is not, when does it occur and when not, how is it expressed and how not, how it could be but is not, and so on.

Problem analysis

This step is about identifying the causes of the problem. Use the helpful demarcation described above with its "is" and "is not" questions.

It is important to work out the characteristics and associated changes and to recognize the connections.

Determine possible causes

The identified characteristics and changes are examined to see how they could have caused the identified problem.

For each possible cause, explain why it is the root cause of the problem, and examine whether all aspects of the problem (description, location, time, scope) can be traced back to it. The most likely cause is the one by which the deviations are best explained.

Summary of the cause analysis

Despite confusing differences, all problems have the same structure. The knowledge of this structure enables us to move from a systematic definition and evaluation to a hypothesis and proof of the cause.

- The **definition** of deviation includes the precise formulation of the undesirable situation whose cause is to be determined.

- The **description** of a problem sets out its dimensions in detail: title, place, time and extent in terms of "what is" and "what is not."

- The **particularities** are identified, i.e., characteristic features of the actual data in all four dimensions.

- The **development of possible causes** starts once all the peculiarities and changes have been identified. All peculiarities and changes are examined for clues to the particular cause.

- The **most likely cause** must explain all the facts in the description.

- The **proof of the most probable cause** should be carried out in practice, that is, through simulation.

Decision analysis/benefit analysis

The decision analysis starts from the **purpose** of the decision, sets the applicable **target criteria** and uses this as basis for the **evaluation** of the alternative in question.

The solution of the decision analysis results from answering these questions:

- For what **purpose**?
- Which **decision-making level** is affected?
- What **effect** should be achieved?
- Which **goal** should be achieved?
- What does the **target state** look like?

Prioritization of the target criteria

- Goals that must be met are mandatory conditions
  (knockout criteria)

- Target objectives that should be met can be achieved differently

Mandatory objectives: These must be met to ensure the success of the decision. Alternatives that do not meet these minimum requirements will not be considered. Mandatory objectives must be measurable.

All other objectives: The developed alternatives are later evaluated according to their relative degree of fulfillment. The target objectives that should be met determine the ranking of the alternatives.

Decide between several alternatives

The decision depends on which alternative or measure suits the objectives best. The ideal alternative brings the best results while at the same time minimizing the necessary effort and minimizing risks. However, ideal alternatives are rare, so the alternatives are judged by their **relative degree of fulfillment** of each individual objective.

For each objective, **multiplying the relative weight by the individual degree of satisfaction** gives the partial benefit of an alternative. The total benefit value of an alternative (the sum of the partial utility values) determines the ranking of the alternatives.

Problem-Solving Form

The results of the problem solving can be summarized as follows:

Objective/subject:
_____

Date and location:

Participants:

Current Situation:

Problem:
Description:

Why is this a problem?

What would the ideal situation look like?

Alternatives:
Option 1:

What are the pros?

What are the cons?
_____

Option 2:

What are the pros?

What are the cons?

Solution:

Action	Detail description	Responsible	Deadline

Epilogue

If you have a good plan and everything goes according to plan, then a project manager does not have much to do.

Change requests, misunderstandings, resource problems, unexpected events, technical and logistical problems, disagreements, etc., can create many tasks for the project manager.

Since these tasks usually have a great impact on the success of the project, it is efficient to prepare, monitor and control routine tasks and operations using checklists and standardized forms.

The project manager can decide according to his/her own priority setting which deviations and tasks require his/her personal attention. He/she can better organize his/her personal time and increase personal effectiveness.

I wish you success in your project work and hope the presented forms and checklists will be useful for you.

You can download many of the presented forms and checklists directly from my homepage, or send me a message if you cannot find the document you need: www.pm-profi.de

Andreas Ketter, November 2018

www.ingramcontent.com/pod-product-compliance
Lightning Source LLC
Chambersburg PA
CBHW051430200326
41520CB00023B/7417